THE GREAT LAKES

Hotel du Nord, Sister Bay, Wisconsin.

COUNTRY INNS OF AMERICA

The Great Lakes

A GUIDE TO THE INNS OF
ILLINOIS, INDIANA, OHIO, MINNESOTA, MICHIGAN, AND WISCONSIN

BY ROBERTA HOMAN GARDNER

PHOTOGRAPHED BY GEORGE W. GARDNER

DESIGNED BY ROBERT REID

HOLT, RINEHART AND WINSTON, *New York*

AN OWL BOOK

Front cover: Victorian Mansion, Galena, Illinois.
Back cover: St. Clair Inn, St. Clair, Michigan.
Frontispiece: A guest room at the Jamieson House, Poynette, Wisconsin.

Maps prepared by Anthony St. Aubyn.
Editorial assistance by Alan Harvey.

Copyright © 1981 by Holt, Rinehart and Winston
All rights reserved, including the right to reproduce
this book or portions thereof in any form.
Published by Holt, Rinehart and Winston,
383 Madison Avenue, New York, New York 10017.
Published simultaneously in Canada by Holt, Rinehart
and Winston of Canada, Limited.

Library of Congress Cataloging in Publication Data
Gardner, Roberta Homan.
   The Great Lakes, a guide to the inns of Illinois,
Indiana, Ohio, Minnesota, Michigan, and Wisconsin.
   (Country inns of America)
   "An Owl book."
   1. Hotels, taverns, etc.—Great Lakes region—
Directories. I. Gardner, George William, 1940–
II. Title. III. Series.
TX907.G34   647′.947701   81-1618
ISBN 0-03-059159-7 (pbk.)   AACR2

First Edition

10 9 8 7 6 5 4 3 2 1

A Robert Reid - Wieser & Weiser Production

Printed in the United States of America

THE INNS

ILLINOIS
- 9   VICTORIAN MANSION, Galena
- 13   COLONIAL GUEST HOUSE, Galena
- 14   EDWARDS GUEST HOUSE, Galena
- 15   RIVERVIEW MANSION HOTEL, Golconda
- 17   HOBSON'S BLUFFDALE, Eldred

INDIANA
- 21   NEW HARMONY INN, New Harmony
- 27   DURBIN HOTEL, Rushville
- 29   SYCAMORE SPRING FARM, Churubusco

OHIO
- 33   DELTA QUEEN, Cincinnati
- 37   THE GOLDEN LAMB, Lebanon
- 41   BUXTON INN, Granville
- 43   BLACKFORK INN, Loudonville

MINNESOTA
- 47   LOWELL INN, Stillwater
- 52   ST. JAMES HOTEL, Red Wing
- 53   ADAMS HOUSE, Mantorville
- 55   THE HOTEL, Winona
- 59   ANDERSON HOUSE, Wabasha
- 61   SCHUMACHER'S NEW PRAGUE HOTEL, New Prague

MICHIGAN
- 65   NATIONAL HOUSE, Marshall
- 69   DEARBORN INN, Dearborn
- 71   BOTSFORD INN, Farmington Hills
- 72   ST. CLAIR INN, St. Clair
- 73   WINDERMERE HOTEL, Mackinac Island
- 75   HOTEL IROQUOIS, Mackinac Island
- 77   STAFFORD'S BAY VIEW, Bay View
- 79   BIRCHWOOD INN, Harbor Springs

WISCONSIN
- 81   JAMIESON HOUSE, Poynette
- 85   OLD RITTENHOUSE INN, Bayfield
- 91   BAY SHORE INN, Sturgeon Bay
- 93   WHITE GULL INN, Fish Creek
- 95   GRIFFIN INN, Ellison Bay
- 96   HOTEL DU NORD, Sister Bay

EDITOR'S NOTE

There are 32 inns described and illustrated in this book. Our photographer and writer visited them all and selected them as outstanding for various reasons: historical interest, food, ambience, innkeepers, furnishings, local amenities. Each inn offers a different mix of characteristics, so study them carefully to determine which ones you might most enjoy. All inngoers have strong personal preferences, and there are inns represented here to suit all tastes.

Visiting a country inn for the first time requires a certain spirit of adventure. Usually an inn is far nicer than we can describe it, but it is also possible for changes to occur since we were there—chefs come and go, staff changes occur—but generally these are temporary, and a visit is usually worthwhile at any time. If not, let us know. And if we have omitted some personal favorites, again let us know so that we can look at them for future editions.

VICTORIAN MANSION

Galena   ILLINOIS

A restoration of unparalleled elegance

After years of indulging their passion for Victorian furniture, Linda and Charles Primrose found the ideal setting for their burgeoning collection. The mid-Victorian Estey mansion had been operated as a guest house but was in serious disrepair. Recognizing that it would perfectly house and complement their acquisitions, they bought the house in 1973 and, after a year of painstaking restoration, opened their doors to guests.

Situated on two acres of partially wooded land, this graceful house in Italianate style offers a wide, welcoming veranda and truly lovely furnishings. It instantly recalls the days of its greatness as the home of a wealthy lead smelter and banker, when its seventeen rooms were often opened to entertain Galena's prominent citizens, among them Ulysses S. Grant.

The focal point of each of the Victorian Mansion's guest rooms is the bed, impressive in brass, chestnut, or walnut and often matched with dresser, wardrobe, or pier glass. For guests' comfort, reading chairs, lamps, and card tables are provided on request.

It is said of Galena that "the hands of the clock stood still at the moment of greatest prosperity." The wealth of the city came from its lead mines, discovered as early as 1693, and from its commercial importance as a major river port. By 1845 it was the wealthiest city in Illinois, but the loss of river traffic to the railroad initiated its decline. Today Galena remains a living monument of Midwest American architecture from the 1820s to the 1870s and boasts more fine examples of early buildings than any other Illinois city. All this contributes greatly to its charm and was a persuasive factor in the Primrose's purchase of this grand mansion.

The Victorian Mansion provides an excellent base

A finely carved chestnut bed.

from which to explore the historic town itself as well as the surrounding Mississippi bluff country, which offers a full range of outdoor sports from hiking and bicycling to wintertime downhill and cross-country skiing.

THE VICTORIAN MANSION, 301 S. High St., Galena, Ill. 61036; (815) 777-0675; Linda and Charles Primrose, Innkeepers. An impeccably furnished Victorian guest house restored to its former grandeur. Open all year except Thanksgiving, Christmas Eve and Day. Five guest rooms with private and shared baths. Rates $18 to $28 single; $20 to $30 double. No meals but restaurants nearby. Children welcome but not encouraged as there is little recreation. No pets. No credit cards. Galena has 11 museums; public swimming pool; historic sites, including home of President Grant; gift shops; art galleries; historic lead mine 6 miles from town; skiing facilities at Chestnut Mountain Resort.

DIRECTIONS: From Chicago, take I-90 northwest to Belvedere U.S.-20 exit. Go west on U.S.-20 to Galena. Cross bridge and drive 4 blocks to High St.; turn right and go 1 block to inn. From Dubuque, take Rte. 20 14 miles to Galena; turn left onto High St. before reaching town. Look for signs marking turn.

Left and front cover. Inside and out, the inn displays the Victorian era in striking style. OVERLEAF. A view of Galena, showing a variety of nineteenth-century architecture.

COLONIAL GUEST HOUSE

Galena — *ILLINOIS*

A historic town, a Greek Revival inn

"People must remember they're going back 100 years when they visit this town. It's just an old, old town," says Mary Keller, owner of the Colonial Guest House. Mary has lived in Galena since childhood and tells some interesting tales.

There is the controversy about the age of the house. It just *may* be the oldest in town, but in any case, it *is* one of Galena's rare Greek Revival houses, with a facade supported by both Ionic and Doric columns. There is no controversy about its having been constructed by Nehemiah Bates, a river merchant, who recorded that when the house was built, the Galena River was 340 feet wide and ran deeper than the Mississippi. As a visitor views the slim finger of river that flows past the house today, it is startling to note that Galena was once an important river port.

The inn's informality makes it a wonderful place to unwind. Mary Keller is a casual innkeeper who enjoys relaxing in front of the television set or over a good book, and her example is infectious. If you are fortunate enough to engage her in conversation, she just might rustle up a cake and coffee snack or a platter of cheese. And although breakfast is advertised as "coffee only," if her schedule permits, she will put out a plate of fresh-baked coffee cake or rolls to be enjoyed on the screened porch shaded by the luxuriant cucumber vines Mary plants each year.

Innkeeper Mary Keller.

The two common rooms on the second floor are furnished with Mary's personal collection of antiques, bric-a-brac, and family photographs. One of her prize possessions is a complete Victorian "cameo" set: six chairs and settee, all with their original rose velvet upholstery. Porcelain figurines, an alabaster bust of Madame de Pompadour, lusterware hurricane lamps, silver services, crystal chandeliers, cranberry glass, and an imposing cherry wardrobe attest to Mary's collecting instincts. But she is also a businesswoman: the ground floor of the house is an antique shop, convenient for leisurely after-breakfast browsing.

There is much for the visitor to see in Galena, where so many buildings and houses, including President Grant's home, have historical associations. During the first weekend in June and the last in September, many private homes are open to public view.

Left and above. Visiting the inn is like walking into an elegant antique shop. A rose velvet settee, china, crystal and a bust of Madame Pompadour are prized possessions.

COLONIAL GUEST HOUSE, 1004 Park Ave., Galena, Ill. 61036; (815) 777-0336; Mrs. Roy (Mary) Keller, Innkeeper. Greek Revival mansion in a historic town. Open all year, but phone ahead in case innkeeper is away. Four guest rooms with private baths, 1 with kitchenette. Rates, including morning coffee, $20 single; $26 double. No meals. Children welcome; pets accepted. No credit cards. Historical Society Museum, Doll and Toy Museum, 1826 miner's trading post restored and furnished in period, Old Stockade and Underground Refuge, Galena Art Theatre, antique and specialty shops, restaurants.

DIRECTIONS: From Chicago, take I-90 northwest to Belvedere U.S.-20 exit. Go west on U.S.-20 to Galena. Turn left on Park Ave. just before bridge crossing. Colonial Guest House is 2nd house from corner. From Dubuque, take U.S.-20 southeast to Galena.

EDWARDS GUEST HOUSE

Galena — ILLINOIS

Friendly hosts bring a small inn to life

The charms of Galena could not receive a finer endorsement than that paid by Ginny and Jerry Edwards. Until July 1980, the Edwards lived in what to many is America's most fabulous city—San Francisco. But on a cross-country trip Ginny fell in love with this historic river town, with its dramatic bluffs and age-softened buildings; and her enthusiasm so infected Jerry that the couple soon moved to heartland Galena.

Within weeks of taking possession of a gracious old white house on the edge of town, the Edwards opened three bedrooms to guests. Each is charmingly old-fashioned in look and feeling, with colorful chintz, antique oak and iron bedsteads, and overhead fans.

An asset to the town, the Edwards bring with them a Western legacy of easygoing friendliness, that essential asset for dedicated innkeepers.

EDWARDS GUEST HOUSE, 713 S. Bench St., Galena, Ill. 61036; (815) 777-1611; Jerry and Ginny Edwards, Innkeepers. The Edwards bring youth and enthusiasm to their task of running this small, informal inn with three double rooms; 1 with bath, other 2 share bath. Open all year. $20 single; $25 to $30 double. No meals but complimentary coffee. Children welcome; pets accepted. No credit cards. For a town its size, Galena has a lot to see, including 11 museums, historic sights, unusual shops, and art galleries. Public swimming pool; skiing facilities nearby.

DIRECTIONS: From Chicago, take I-90 to Belvedere U.S.-20 exit. Go west on U.S.-20 to Galena. Cross bridge, take first left. Guest House is last house on block. From Dubuque, take U.S.-20 east to Galena. Go to Bench St. and turn right to last house on block.

Innkeepers Jerry and Ginny Edwards on the balcony.

Golconda RIVERVIEW MANSION HOTEL
ILLINOIS

A lively hotel in a sleepy town

Innkeeper Carole Brown is one of those remarkable people—part genius, part human dynamo—who conceive and then do all the dirty work to create an institution. Her particular institution is the imposing Riverview Mansion Hotel, a former private home overlooking the banks of the Ohio River.

After teaching English at a university, Carole decided she wanted to get away from "the ivory tower and into real work." She bought this historic hotel, and "real work" it was. Renovating on a shoestring, Carole has gotten off to an impressive start. When completed, the inn promises all the amenities and meanwhile offers guests abundant charm and all the flavor of a real "country inn."

Once the home of a wealthy businessman, the Riverview contains many of the original furnishings and antiques. Ma Barker's, the rustic lunch room, is presided over by an accomplished cook, locally famous for old-fashioned country cooking.

The town of Golconda, in the Shawnee National Forest, is an ideal stopping place from which to visit the many scenic wonders of southeastern Illinois.

THE RIVERVIEW MANSION HOTEL, Box 56, Columbus Ave., Golconda, Ill. 62938; (618) 685-3001; Carole Brown, Innkeeper. A spacious hostelry in a quiet Ohio River town. Open all year. Twelve guest rooms; 2 apartments. Private and shared baths. Rates $16 single; $20 double. Restaurant, open to public, serves 3 meals a day except Mondays. Children welcome; pets accepted. No credit cards. Recreational possibilities are endless in this scenic area. Archeological sites, bird watching, hunting, fishing, country auctions, boating; Bicentennial bike path passes in front of hotel; bikers may camp in backyard.

DIRECTIONS: From Chicago, take I-57 south to I-24. Continue on 24 to Rte. 146; turn left to Golconda. At Columbus Ave., just past courthouse, turn right. Hotel 2 blocks down on left.

HOBSON'S BLUFFDALE
Eldred — ILLINOIS

A working farm where city folk flourish

Define a country inn, place it in America's heartland, give it a new twist, and you have Hobson's Bluffdale—a vacation retreat that is also a busy working farm nestled in the Mississippi and Illinois River valley. One hour's drive north of St. Louis, Bill and Lindy Hobson's farm is a great place to unwind and discover the joy of just doin' what comes naturally.

This farmland has been in the family for seven generations, and for fascinating reading of that past there is the Hobsons' copy of great-grandfather's revealing chronicle of *his* father's life and that of the surrounding area.

Guests are encouraged to take part in the farm chores, float on a raft in the pool, take a picnic lunch to the river, go horseback riding, or visit Northwestern University's archeological dig three miles away. This area is rich in Indian history, and a stroll through the woods might turn up an Indian tool or arrowhead.

Breakfast, lunch, and dinner are served family style at long dining tables, where guests sit elbow to elbow and pass heaping bowls and platters. The farm's produce provides fresh fruits, vegetables, eggs, and fresh sausage or slab bacon on each day's menu. Fresh hams, pork chops, ribs and Lindy's fried chicken, pies, and homemade ice cream awaken tired taste buds. Lindy's baked goods are famous, and she gives lessons in bread making and preserving jams and jellies. Once a week the Hobsons roast a whole hog, have an early morning trail breakfast, and organize a boating picnic.

Visits from relatives gave the Hobsons the idea of opening a guest house. Children were always especially reluctant to leave, and now it is commonplace for guests to sign up a child to stay an additional week or even an entire summer. The Hobsons' four strapping sons take their responsibilities seriously and set their young guests a fine example.

Though short on glamour, the farm provides its own kind of comfort. The bunkhouse was designed to accommodate families; each room has its own bath and suites afford the privacy of two separate rooms. The Hobsons offer a rare experience in living, and their outgoing nature reflects their personal honest and warm generosity.

A better vacation would be hard to find.

HOBSON'S BLUFFDALE, Rte. 1, Eldred, Ill. 62027; (217) 983-2854; Bill and Lindy Hobson, Innkeepers. In the main house, centerpiece of the farm, are dining room, TV room, and telephone. Air-conditioned guest rooms with private baths in nearby bunkhouse. Three suites, 2 bedrooms each; 4 family rooms, housing up to 4 persons; 1 single. Rates, per person, including 3 meals a day, $30, weekly $190; children 8 to 11, $22.50, weekly $140; under 8, $17, weekly $100. Day rate, meals, and recreation $15. Write for group rates and package plans. No pets; no credit cards. Recreation includes sharing farm chores: gardening, berry picking, etc. Riding, swimming, canoeing, square dancing, pony cart and hayrides; picnics, boat trips, haymow with rope swing, playhouse.

DIRECTIONS: From St. Louis, take I-270 north to Rte. 367 and Alton where it becomes Rte. 67. Just north of Alton, take Rte. 267 to Carrollton; turn left on Rte. 108. Drive approximately 8 miles to Eldred. Turn right at bottom of hill and drive 3.7 miles to farm.

Left and below. The rural life, where a vacation with the Hobsons is "like visiting relatives." OVERLEAF. The barn by day, with author Roberta Gardner, left, and another guest heading for the open range.

NEW HARMONY INN

New Harmony — INDIANA

A place of great social expectations

"I cannot explain with words how gladly and well I live in this pleasant New World. The woods are green, the herbs are growing.... Flowers bloom in our gardens.... It is surely a joy to live here." So wrote German-born George Rapp in a letter from New Harmony, the religious community he and his disciples established in 1814 on the banks of the Wabash River. In pursuit of new challenges, the Rappites sold their community in 1825 to Robert Owen, British industrialist and social reformer. With his partner William Maclure, Owen organized a group of intellectuals and teachers to build "a new and better world" through "universal education." Though it failed as a utopian society, New Harmony can take credit for having been the birthplace of the kindergarten, free public schools, trade schools, women's clubs, public libraries, and the first geological survey.

Genius is preserved and celebrated in New Harmony. Buildings used as dormitories by Rapp and as schools by Owen are meticulously tended. Rappite log cabins and the cemetery of unmarked graves stand silently side by side. And dramatic modern architecture by noted designers Philip Johnson and Richard Meier adds a powerful dimension that keeps the town from being locked into the past.

Accommodations at the New Harmony Inn are in the Residence, where many of the forty-five guest rooms have woodburning fireplaces and balconies overlooking a country pond. The Studio House, a simple Rappite-style dwelling, sleeps a family of four. Then, in a league by itself, there is Orchard House. Jane Blaffer Owen, wife of a direct descendant of Robert Owen, and a person devoted to New Harmony, has decorated Orchard House with priceless antiques and works of art; professors and writers in need of a quiet place to work often choose to stay here, but it is also a house for special occasions.

Two restaurants serve the inn. The Red Geranium is a rambling clapboard house that prides itself on its cuisine; a favorite entrée is the Texas-style char prime steak, a charcoal-grilled slab of prime rib. The Shadblow, featuring lighter fare, is a short walk into town.

Left. The Orchard House dining room basks in the late afternoon sun. OVERLEAF. "The Residence," as the new inn buildings are called. Following is an Orchard House guest room—light, cheerful, and sumptuous, with an original Audubon.

The Rappite-style Studio House.

Whether the utopians instilled this place with magic, or its magnetism was there first to attract them, New Harmony remains more than ever an oasis for both body and spirit.

THE NEW HARMONY INN, Box 581, North St., New Harmony, Ind. 47631; (812) 682-4491; Gary J. Gerard, Manager. An inn as harmonious as the town it graces. Forty-five rooms, 2 houses; private baths. Open all year. Rates $30 to $55 single; $37 to $60 double; children under 12 no charge. Studio House sleeps 4, $100. Orchard House (applicants must be screened) $340. Red Geranium Restaurant, open to public, serves lunch and dinner. Closed Mondays, Christmas Day, New Year's Day, and July 4. Shadblow Restaurant serves 3 meals daily except Christmas. Children welcome; no pets. MasterCard, Visa, American Express, Diners Club, Carte Blanche credit cards accepted. Heated indoor swimming pool, tennis courts in town, golf privileges at Country Club; New Harmony tour of 12 exhibition buildings and historic sites.

DIRECTIONS: From Chicago, take U.S.-41 south to Rte. 68 exit. Go south on 68 to Rte. 6. Turn right on 66 and drive 1 mile to New Harmony. Turn right at stoplight and drive 2 blocks. From St. Louis, take I-64 to Poseyville, Ind., exit. Turn south onto Rte. 68.

DURBIN HOTEL

Rushville — INDIANA

A nostalgia trip to the 1940s

Midwest small-town life is elevated to an art at the Durbin Hotel. It is the heartbeat of Rushville, a town bypassed by merchandisers of the quaint and cute. Years of accommodating to the ebb and flow of town life has left its mark on this institution. It is simple, unpretentious, and well loved by the local citizenry.

Back in 1940, Wendell Willkie, Republican candidate for president and a Rushville native, made the Durbin his campaign headquarters. For five months the hotel buzzed with excitement and Rushville was on the map. The Wendell Willkie lounge in one corner of the lobby, presided over by his portrait in oil, commemorates those stirring days.

May and Leo Durbin bought the hotel in 1928 and raised a family there. Today David Durbin manages the hotel for members of the business community who bought it in January 1980. Dave loves the town and the hotel. As he puts it, "Once innkeeping is in your blood, it's hard to shake." He is a gentleman innkeeper, interested in everyone who walks through the door, with a sincere, ready smile for all.

The new owners are sprucing up the hotel with a new paint job and some major remodeling. It is hoped that they do not change its character too drastically. For those nostalgic for the 1950s, a walk through the lobby is a rewarding experience. The formica check-in desk and "modern" furniture are a perfect counterpoint to the Willkie lounge, where the atmosphere is a bit like Sunday at grandma's.

The guest rooms range from charming, with an-

The Willkie Lounge.

tique bedsteads and dressers, to quite plain. But plain or fancy, many rooms offer that vanishing luxury Magic Fingers—a vibrating mattress—as well as television, telephone, and complimentary coffee.

Dining at the Durbin is an inexpensive pleasure. Specialties of the house include locally raised chicken and pork, bacon-wrapped filet mignon, and a few Chinese-inspired dishes. There is a well-stocked salad bar at lunch and dinner and superb yeast rolls—cinnamon at breakfast and dinner rolls with other meals. In addition the full-time baker makes such satisfying desserts as sugar cream pie and chocolate cake with butterscotch icing.

Rushville is off the beaten track. But for the traveler in search of a respite from the phony and flamboyant, it is worth a visit. The Durbin is "American naïve" in a world of increasing sophistication.

The dining area.
Left. The guest rooms are especially cozy and charmingly decorated.

DURBIN HOTEL, 137 W. Second St., Rushville, Ind. 46173; (317) 932-4161; David Durbin, Innkeeper. Typical American small-town hotel; pleasant exterior painted cream with forest green trim and shutters, wrought-iron balcony. Open all year. Restaurant closed Christmas Day and New Year's Day. Twenty-eight rooms with baths; some tubs, some showers; TV and telephones. Rates $17.50 to $21 single; $20 to $27.50 double; suite $40. Children and pets welcome. MasterCard, Visa, American Express, Carte Blanche, Diners Club credit cards accepted. Rushville has little to offer in the way of recreation. Plans to open athletic club in 1982 with racquetball, exercise room, health club facilities. Metamora, 18 miles away, an arts and crafts town with galleries, canal and locks, old mill. Brookville Reservoir, a 30-mile drive, has boating and picnic grounds.

DIRECTIONS: From Indianapolis, take I-74 east to Rte. 44 (second Shelbyville exit). Drive 18 miles to Rushville. From Cincinnati, take I-74 west to Rte. 3, Rushville exit at Greensburg. Turn right on Rte. 3 and go 18 miles to Rushville. At courthouse turn left 1 block. From Columbus, take I-70 west to Rte. 3; turn left and drive 18 miles to Rushville. At courthouse turn right 1 block.

SYCAMORE SPRING FARM

Churubusco — INDIANA

Hoosier hospitality on a "beefalo" farm

Janice McCoy grew up in the shadow of Williamsburg. Husband Jerry is a gentleman farmer, who reads Jefferson and raises "beefalo." Together they have created a little world of simplicity and order—a picture-book farm that by will and whim pays homage to the past.

When their barn burned, Jerry designed another with an original construction plan. Afterward, he says, "I found an old book on barns and a design just like the one I had done. It was an ancient design, made to suit a need, just like mine. This discovery really made me feel a connection with the past."

When they were building their house, a structure inspired by Williamsburg architecture, Jerry met with restorers who gave him needed information to ensure authenticity. Special knives were made to carve moldings, and the pine flooring, secured with exposed square-headed nails, was taken from an old Philadelphia house. The family room and formal living room have large, efficient fireplaces, built after the designs of American scientist and inventor Count Rumford. A handsome screened porch faces Janice's garden and the rolling meadows where the beefalo roam, and serves as a dining room in clement weather.

The three daily meals, served family style, display Janice's considerable talents. Beefalo-burgers, grilled on the porch, are served with fresh-picked corn on the cob and garden salad with tomatoes warm from the sun. Other specialties include beef curry with noodles, lemon-barbequed chicken, Hoosier fried chicken, fresh-baked Sally Lunn, Dutch apple crumb pie, and pound cake à la mode topped with homemade fudge sauce.

Since guest accommodations at the farm are limited, reservations are advised. There are no organized activities, but there is plenty to do in the neighborhood. Chain-O-Lakes State Park is nearby, and country auctions offer occasional bargains. And the Amish settlement of Shipshewana is fascinating; there visitors can wander through fruit and vegetable markets or buy fine Amish yard goods. If you feel like helping out on the farm, there is berry picking and jam-and-bread making with Janice.

Or perhaps you might prefer to sunbathe on a raft in the pond, or read on the porch, or just plain loaf!

The farmhouse is authentic Williamsburg, from its Virginia gambrel roof and bedroom dormer windows, *above*, to the paned windows and mouldings, *left*. OVERLEAF. Driving up to the inn, it is a delight to see a well-ordered successful family farm in its prime.

SYCAMORE SPRING FARM, Box 224, Churubusco, Ind. 46723; (219) 693-3603; Jerry and Janice McCoy, Innkeepers. Enjoy country life at this working Midwestern farm. Two guest rooms house 8 persons for 2-day minimum stay. Private baths. Reservations advised. Rates $40 per person per day, children 12 and under $20; rates include 3 meals. No pets; no credit cards. Swimming, fishing in farm pond; 5 minutes from state park with canoeing, fishing, swimming, nature trails.

DIRECTIONS: From Chicago, take I-94 east to I-65; go south to U.S.-30 at Merrillville. Take U.S.-30 east to Rte. 9 at Columbia City. Drive north on 9 approximately 11 miles (1½ miles past blinker light at U.S.-33 intersection). Turn right on Rte. 300 south for 2 miles. Turn right on Rte. 200 east. Lane is 1st on left at split-rail fence. From Fort Wayne, take U.S.-33 north to Churubusco. Go through town to 2nd crossroad (look for sign The Farm), turn right 3 miles to split-rail fence.

DELTA QUEEN

Cincinnati — OHIO

A floating inn from the steamboat era

The Dixieland jazz combo is indefatigable.

"She was a grand affair. Here was a sumptuous glass temple with room enough to have a dance in. She was clean and dainty as a drawing room. The bar was marvelous and the barkeeper had been barbered and upholstered at incredible cost," wrote Mark Twain in *Life on the Mississippi*.

Today steamboatin' is alive on the *Delta Queen*. This paddlewheel masterpiece tours the Ohio and Mississippi Rivers from Cincinnati to New Orleans and from New Orleans up to St. Paul, "locking through" the Mississippi's twenty-six locks. The leisurely pace ensures relaxation. There are no schedules to keep, no baggage to carry, no restaurants to seek out. It is all on board, where a trained crew makes everything work like a fine watch.

Listed on the National Register of Historic Places, the *Delta Queen* has an exterior "wedding cake" charm that is matched by interior elegance. Rich mahogany and oak posts and paneling complement burnished brass stair rails and fittings; stained glass windows and the Orleans Room's Siamese ironbark floor bespeak irreplaceable quality. White and gold bedrooms provide comfort, privacy, and most command a river view.

Life on board is both exciting and tranquil. At sailing time the calliope toots out steamy choruses, from "Camptown Races" to "Bill Bailey"; on board, the Riverboat Ramblers keep things jumping with Dixieland, bluegrass, ragtime, and dance music every night.

The *Delta Queen* makes many shore stops with time for passengers to tour such historic towns as Memphis, Natchez, and Hannibal, Missouri. Kite flying, classic movies, sunbathing, or just watching the shores glide by occupy the leisurely hours.

The boat's galley offers abundance and variety. Crabmeat Louis, Arkansas catfish, Bay Street tournedos with *marchand de vin* sauce make frequent appearances along with such irresistible desserts as key lime pie, crème de menthe parfait, and peach Melba. Early risers are accommodated with morning coffee at six o'clock, and night owls find the late buffet open at eleven.

As she steams the great rivers, today's passengers experience the nostalgic pleasure of what the *Delta Queen* was always meant to be: a magnificent overnight passenger steamboat.

Each night a chambermaid turns down the bed and leaves a sweet.
Left. The "Delta Queen" glides past Cincinnati's Riverfront stadium. OVERLEAF. The stern wheeler in all her glory.

DELTA QUEEN, 511 Main St., Cincinnati, Ohio 45202; (800) 543-1949; in Ohio (800) 582-1888; Henry Mitchell, Chief Purser. America's palatial Mississippi River hotel operates Feb. through Dec. Rates range from $145 for a 2-night round-trip cruise from New Orleans to $2095 for a 10-night cruise from Cincinnati or St. Louis to New Orleans, including all meals. For a complete list of rates and a variety of cruises, consult your travel agent or write for handsome illustrated color brochure. Children welcome; no pets. American Express credit card accepted.

DIRECTIONS: In Cincinnati ship docks at Public Landing, foot of Broadway. In St. Louis at foot of Gateway Arch. In St. Paul at Lambert St. landing. In New Orleans at International Passenger Terminal.

THE GOLDEN LAMB

Lebanon — OHIO

Charles Dickens would like it better today

"Picket fence and Victorian with a Shaker influence," is innkeeper Jackson Reynolds's thumbnail description of this inn, which is, in fact, listed as a Shaker museum. Today's mellowed red brick building replaces an earlier log tavern and dates from 1815. Ohio's oldest inn, it houses an impressive collection of antiques, including superb examples of priceless Shaker furniture, much of it still in daily use.

Lebanon was an important stagecoach stop, and the inn has played host to ten presidents as well as to such luminaries as Mark Twain, Henry Clay, Daniel Webster, and Charles Dickens, who by the way did not find it to his liking. He complained bitterly that he was forced to drink tea or coffee: "As they are both very bad, and the water worse, I ask for brandy but it is a temperance hotel, and spirits were not to be had for love or money." Today, brandy and other potables may be had in the Black Horse Tavern.

Dining at the Golden Lamb is a special delight for lovers of fine American fare. The appetizer tray might offer hominy and chick pea relish, watermelon pickle, and egg salad. Entrées may include roast leg of spring lamb, country fried chicken, roast Long Island duckling, stuffed pork chops with Shaker apple dressing, and roast turkey. Two full-time bakers turn out delicious breads and desserts.

Though the dining room is closed Christmas Day, festivities are in order during the rest of the holiday season. Guests may take a glass of eggnog while enjoying the decorations, the roaring fire, and cheerful carols played on a Regina music box or sung by the Dickens Carolers, who wear period costumes and entertain in the dining rooms. The menu may feature a wassail bowl, innkeeper's pâté, and venison, Smithfield ham, or braised goose and stuffing.

The guest rooms occupy most of the top three floors. The elegant Charles Dickens Room has a replica of Lincoln's massive and ornate bed, and the DeWitt Clinton Room houses a signed Boyd bed. Each room combines the solid comfort of earlier days with such modern amenities as television and telephones.

A collection of Shaker furniture is displayed in the Shaker dining room.

Left. A signed Boyd bed occupies the DeWitt Clinton guest room. OVERLEAF. A room dedicated to Sarah Stubbs, a little girl who lived at the inn in the mid-1800s, is filled with old-fashioned toys.

THE GOLDEN LAMB, 27 S. Broadway, Lebanon, Ohio 45036; (513) 932-5065; Jackson B. Reynolds, Innkeeper. Ohio's oldest inn, the Golden Lamb has been host for over two centuries to many celebrities. Furnished with fine antiques, including a rare collection of Shaker furniture. All but one of the 18 guest rooms have private baths. All have TV sets. Open all year; dining rooms closed Christmas Day. The inn's Black Horse Tavern serves drinks; the dining rooms serve lunch and dinner daily, breakfast Sunday only. For weekly breakfasts, the Village Ice Cream Parlor opposite inn recommended. Rates $28 to $32 single; $32 to $36 double; Dickens Room $45. Children welcome; no pets. MasterCard, Visa, American Express, Diners Club credit cards accepted. Inn's Lamb Shop has gifts for young and old. There is much to see in Lebanon; the Warren County Historical Society two doors from inn has a restored 19th-century village with displays, shops, and costumed mannequins. Glendower State Museum is a carefully preserved Greek Revival home. An hour's drive from the inn, the Air Force Museum displays a large collection of historic and modern aircraft. Antiquing is a popular local recreation. Ask innkeeper for best shops.

DIRECTIONS: From Cincinnati, take I-75 north to Lebanon exit Rte. 63. Turn right 5 miles to parking lot behind inn. Inn is 45 miles from downtown Cincinnati. From Dayton, take I-75 south; turn left on Rte. 63. Inn is 35 miles from downtown Dayton.

BUXTON INN

Granville — OHIO

Fine food and hospitality, and a ghostly "lady in blue"

For nearly a century this beautifully restored inn has been dispensing genial hospitality. Built in 1812 and in operation ever since, it has played host to many illustrious guests. Because of its brace-and-beam construction, pegged walnut floors and frames, and original windows, Henry Ford is said to have coveted it for his Greenfield Village Restoration. Now in the National Register of Historic Places, the Buxton is a source of pride to Granville residents.

The inn's stunning exterior is painted a dramatic "Buxton peach," strikingly set off by forest green shutters and doors. White double-deck porches run the length of the building, softly illuminated by glass and tin box lanterns. The inn's sign commemorates Major Buxton, a cat that once reigned at the inn and is immortalized as its trademark.

Age-old standards of excellence are maintained today by owners and innkeepers Audrey and Orville Orr.

Since the inn has only three guest rooms (reservations are essential), its reputation rests largely on the quality of its cuisine. The dining room is open to all for lunch and dinner, served by waitresses in floor-length gingham dresses, white aprons, and ruffled caps.

Popular entrées include Louisiana chicken with artichoke hearts and almonds; French pepper steak with brandy; and a fine selection of fresh fish, such as red snapper with lump crabmeat and a light Béarnaise sauce, curried halibut, and coquille of seafood Cardinal. Light eaters might choose a shrimp and orange salad; cold vegetables vinaigrette; or watercress salad garnished with pears, oranges, and tomatoes. A well-stocked cellar provides wines to complement any meal. Rich and delectable final touches include Daisy Hunter's hot walnut fudge cake, peach Melba, hot pistachio cake à la mode, and double-dark chocolate cake.

While enjoying an evening at the inn, guests might catch a glimpse of its kindly resident ghost, a "lady in blue," said to be a former owner and light opera star. Innkeeper Orr claims to have seen the lady, though she appears infrequently.

Each guest room has a private outside entrance. Sleigh beds and a silver chandelier grace one; another features nineteenth-century Eastlake furniture. The third is a two-room suite with elegant Victorian beds, velvet settee, crystal chandelier, and Oriental rugs.

Hospitality, colonial charm, fine food, and efficient service all combine to make the Buxton well worth a visit.

Color at the Buxton is adventurous, as these guest rooms indicate.

THE BUXTON INN, 313 E. Broadway, Granville, Ohio 43023; (614) 587-0001; Audrey and Orville Orr, Innkeepers. A charming inn where the emphasis is on fine food. Open all year. Three guest rooms with private baths. Single $28.50; double $32.50. Dining room serves lunch and dinner only; open to public by reservation. Closed Christmas Eve, Christmas Day, New Year's Day, July 4. Breakfast available at nearby recommended restaurant. Children welcome; no pets. MasterCard, Visa credit cards accepted. Dennison University presents films, theater, lectures. Skiing nearby. Hopewell Indian earthworks 5 miles; Owens-Corning research center and glassware museum in Newark.

DIRECTIONS: From Columbus, take I-70 to Rte. 37 Granville exit; drive north 9 miles to stoplight. Turn right 3 blocks. From Cleveland, take I-71 south to Rte. 13 Mansfield exit. Drive south on 13 to Mt. Vernon; then take Rte. 661, bearing right in Mt. Vernon to Granville. Turn left at stoplight.

BLACKFORK INN

Loudonville — OHIO

Victoriana without clutter in a gracious Ohio inn

"When you walk into a bedroom here, I feel it is the closest thing to Victorian times, outside a museum," said Joe Pittenger, co-innkeeper with wife, Janine, of the Blackfork. After several years as a deep-sea diver in Europe, Joe dreamed of running a bed-and-breakfast styled after those in France, England, and Scotland. The dream took shape when he saw a For Sale sign on a distinctive mansard-roofed Victorian house in his hometown of Loudonville. The Pittengers promptly bought it and began an exhaustive study of the Victorian era, which took them to London's Victoria and Albert Museum for a firsthand look at authentic examples of the period.

One of the museum's curators discovered working blueprints for a hotel in Bath built in 1865, the same year the Pittengers' house was built. Back home, they studied the plans and many books on the subject. With Joe as general contractor and Janine as designer, they created a charming Victorian inn that avoids the overly decorated aspects of Victorian decor. The Blackfork is a toned-down version, pleasantly devoid of clutter. Each guest room reflects a different mood and each is furnished with antiques bought in England and Scotland. Only the beds, many of them brass, and the Victorian light fixtures are reproductions. The bathrooms deserve special mention for their reproductions of old-time, overhead chain-pull oak water tanks and oak toilet seats, washbasin rims, and towel racks.

The bill of fare at the Blackfork deserves high marks. Joe's favorite meal is breakfast, which he boasts is "fit for a king." An uncommon touch, breakfast is served until two o'clock for the benefit of late sleeping guests. In addition to the usual morning fare, the menu offers such delectable dishes as Teresa's Eggs, a combination of creamed spinach, artichoke hearts, and poached eggs, topped with a light and buttery hollandaise sauce. Chicken livers Malabar are gently sautéed and served with fresh mushrooms and a flavorful wine sauce. Lunch includes salads and sandwiches; the dinner menu emphasizes beef and seafood. Alternatively, dinner guests may phone ahead and create their own menu within guidelines proffered by the chef, Joe's father, a professional once voted one of the nation's ten best.

Janine and Joe admire the slower pace of European life, and at the Blackfork this relaxed way of life prevails.

BLACKFORK INN, 303 N. Water St., Loudonville, Ohio 44842; (419) 994-3252; Janine and Joe Pittenger, Innkeepers. Painstaking research went into the restoration and decoration of this 6-room Victorian inn that avoids the garishness and clutter of the period. Inn located in the heart of Ohio's picturesque Amish country. Open all year. Rates $58 to $68, double; $50 single, with full breakfast. Private baths. Cable TV with HBO available. Children welcome; no pets. MasterCard and Visa credit cards accepted. Mohican State Park has hiking trails, cross-country skiing, canoeing. Louis Bromfield's Malabar Farm nearby. Antiquing and excellent restaurants in Loudonville and surrounding area.

DIRECTIONS: From Cleveland, take I-71 south to U.S.-250 exit. Turn right 3 miles to center of Ashland. Turn left on Rte. 60 and drive approximately 20 miles to Loudonville. At first stoplight turn left 2 blocks. From Columbus, take I-71 north to Sunbury exit, Rtes. 36, 37. Turn right 3 miles to first stoplight. Turn left on Rte. 3 and drive approximately 35 miles to Loudonville. At first stoplight turn left and at next light turn right 1½ blocks to inn.

Left. The inviting dining room, with its lovely woodwork, rose velvet chairs, and fresh flowers. OVERLEAF. The green and red Victorian suite, left, contains a massive armoire and velvet love seat; right, a brass bed with one-quarter canopy is framed by rich floral wallpaper.

LOWELL INN

Stillwater — MINNESOTA

Where the art of innkeeping reaches a peak of perfection

Three elements make the Lowell Inn one of the finest hostelries in America: attentive service, impeccable food, and stunning decor.

To the elder Palmers, parents of Art Palmer, the present innkeeper, good service was taken for granted, good food was a necessity, and good taste a matter of instinct. Their instincts were right; they were inveterate and discerning collectors, who knew and acquired the finest in furniture, porcelain, silver, and objets d'art, all of which adorn the inn today.

Built in 1930, the Lowell's classic colonial architecture makes it look much older. The front portico is supported by thirteen columns, representing the original colonies and bearing their flags. In the lobby Williamsburg and French Provincial meet harmoniously. This melding of decorative contrasts carries over into the guest rooms, but still, some of the baths are a surprise: Roman and Greek fantasies with bath and shower "in the round," complemented by modern jacuzzis!

Contrasts persist, too, in the three dining rooms — from the informal Garden Room to the stately George Washington Room with its Capo di Monte porcelain, Sheffield silver services, and Dresden china collections on the sideboards. (Even the menus are printed on porcelain.)

But the most spectacular dining is in the Matterhorn Room, dedicated to Arthur and Maureen Palmer's Swiss heritage and to the art of Swiss woodcarving. In addition to their personal collection of the work of old masters, there is the artistry of a contemporary Swiss carver brought to Lowell Inn by the Palmers. Here he created beautiful doors and furniture, and the pièce de résistance, a wall mural of the Matterhorn carved in grainless African white mahogany.

Meals at the inn are simple and delicious. Art

Palmer is a perfectionist who uses more than 2,000 suppliers of the finest produce. In Switzerland he tasted a particularly pleasing coffee, of which he is now the sole importer. An entire Swiss vineyard's crop of Merlot rosé, on the vine in October, is delivered to the inn and served in December.

Palmer reflects on innkeeping: "It's an art to know how far to go with detail. To know what is too much and pull back an inch. The point is to create the unexpected. To allow people to make discoveries each time they visit."

At the Lowell this magic formula works.

LOWELL INN, 102 N. 2nd St., Stillwater, Minn. 55082; (612) 439-1100; Arthur and Maureen Palmer and Mary Palmer Simon, Innkeepers. A handsome colonial style inn in the beautiful St. Croix valley. Open all year. Twenty-one guest rooms with private baths, some with jacuzzis. Overnight rates, double occupancy only, Palmer French Provincial Suite $129; Bridal and Anniversary $99; Deluxe King and Queen $69, $79, $89; Petite Queen $59. Three dining rooms serve 3 meals a day; open to public for lunch and dinner. Closed Thanksgiving and Christmas Day. Children welcome; no pets. MasterCard, Visa, and American Express credit cards accepted. Many recreational activities in St. Croix valley; canoeing on river, swimming, game preserve, tennis, golf course 8 miles from inn; Washington County Historical Society maintains 3 museums in area. Stillwater has historic restorations and quaint shops.

DIRECTIONS: Forty minutes from Minneapolis/St. Paul. Take I-94 east to Lakeland; go north on Rte. 95 to Stillwater. From downtown, turn left one block at second stoplight.

Left. The portrait of founder Arthur Palmer, Sr. is flanked by Venetian lusters from wife Nelle's collection. OVERLEAF. Left, above, the china cabinet in the George Washington dining room contains Nelle Palmer's fine collection of Venetian glass, Dresden china and priceless Capo di Monte porcelain. Below, one of the exotic, luxurious bedrooms with its unique color scheme and, right, the lobby sitting room features French silk curtains gathered into carved gold-leafed valances. Following are two fantasy bedrooms with Italian jacuzzi baths and matched linens. A porcelain cat greets guests in each room.

ST. JAMES HOTEL

Red Wing — MINNESOTA

Historic hostelry catering to travelers since the 1870s

In 1875 the port of Red Wing on the Mississippi was the world's largest major wheat market. To accommodate visitors in a manner befitting the town's prominence, local businessmen anted up money to build a luxury hotel conveniently situated for rail and steamboat travelers. Its food was so renowned that the railroad changed its timetable to allow passengers a stopover just to enjoy a meal.

Today, 106 years later, this landmark has been restored to its original glory, with an added dimension. The hotel is now the centerpiece of a shopping mall bustling with activity. The lobby and dining room, furnished with Victorian reproductions, recall its original opulence. Contemporary luxuries include complimentary champagne and TV in each guest room as well as a chambermaid, armed with extra bath towels, who turns back the bedclothes in the evening.

The founding fathers would be proud.

ST. JAMES HOTEL, 406-416 Main St., Red Wing, Minn. 55066; (612) 388-2846; Eugene Foster, General Manager. An attractively restored, Italianate red brick hotel, now on National Register of Historic Places. Open all year. Forty-one guest rooms with private baths, cable TV, telephones. $29.50 single; $39.50 to $65 double. Formal Victorian dining room and coffee shop serving 3 meals a day open to public. Children welcome; no pets. MasterCard, Visa, American Express credit cards accepted. Situated on a beautiful stretch of the Mississippi River, outdoor activities abound. Fishing, boating, golf, tennis, skiing, historic sites. YMCA with indoor swimming pool nearby.

DIRECTIONS: From Minneapolis/St. Paul, take U.S.-52 south to Hastings exit; go east on Rte. 55 to Hastings, then south on U.S.-61 to Red Wing. At 4th stoplight turn left ½ block to parking garage.

The Fireside Study off the lobby.

Mantorville — MINNESOTA

ADAMS HOUSE

Buy a guided tour and get a room free

"I'm a hassle remover is what I am." Mary Rose Van Poperin, innkeeper of the Adams House, does not rent rooms; she rents a guide service and throws in a night's stay. Familiarity with southeastern Minnesota and skills as driver, art teacher, and ski instructor are her strong points; and she willingly acts as partner and guide for tennis, canoeing, bicycling, and antiquing. She will even drop hikers off at the start of a trail and meet them at the finish with cold drinks and sandwiches.

Guests at the nineteenth-century Adams House share a communal breakfast at the dining table. For other meals the Hubbell House, an 1854 landmark restaurant, is worth a visit.

Prospective guests must apply in advance, giving dates of proposed visit, activities of interest, relationship of people in party, and two references.

"My guests tend to get very involved," says Mary Rose. "I want them to feel that this is their home in the country."

THE ADAMS HOUSE, Box 252, 220 W. 6th St., Mantorville, Minn. 55955; (507) 635-5406, 635-5132; Mary Rose Van Poperin, Hostess. This Greek Revival townhouse is open all year. Four guest rooms share bath. Rates $16 per person; $30 for 2, including "glorified" continental breakfast. These rates pay for Ms. Van Poperin's guide services and/or lessons, and in addition guests pay her expenses for gasoline, lunch, etc. Persons staying elsewhere in the area may also employ her services. Write for charge sheet and application form with special weekend rates for Minneapolis/St. Paul residents. Children over 8 welcome; no pets. No credit cards. Countryside around Mantorville beautiful, ideal for hiking and bicycling. Croquet, 9-hole golf course, tennis, swimming, fishing, canoeing, summer theater, sightseeing, skiing.

DIRECTIONS: From Minneapolis/St. Paul, take U.S.-52 south to Hader. Exit onto Rte. 57; go south to Mantorville. From Rochester, go west on U.S.-14 to Kasson; exit north onto Rte. 57 to Mantorville.

THE HOTEL

Winona — MINNESOTA

Modern amenities in Mark Twain country

"The majestic bluffs that overlook the river . . . charm one with the grace and variety of their forms, and the soft beauty of their adornment. And then you have the shining river . . . interrupted at intervals by clusters of wooded islands threaded by silver channels, and it is as tranquil and reposeful as dreamland and has nothing this-worldly about it—nothing to hang a fret or worry upon." So wrote Mark Twain on seeing the northern Mississippi River valley.

Lumbering, Winona's first industry, brought wealth and progress to the town, and by 1892 the Schlitz Hotel, built by the famed Milwaukee family, was home to travelers. Noted for its billiard and smoking rooms, as well as for its excellent food, the hotel flourished until the Depression. It was rescued from decay only a few years ago.

Today the meticulously restored hotel is a fine modern hostelry, spanking clean and graciously decorated with reproduction Victorian furniture upholstered in soft shades of peach, green, and blue. The second floor lobby has a skylight that illuminates the public rooms, an enormous theater scrim on the stairway landing, the handsome oak banisters, and the intricate, pressed-metal ceiling. Arriving guests are greeted by the charming concierge Meta Weiss who proffers a bottle of chilled champagne.

Zach's Restaurant in the hotel serves the best food in town, offering such specialties as king crabmeat in wine sauce, veal Oscar with fresh asparagus, and roast duck à l'orange.

Graceful candelabra fill the dining room with a soft glow, and silk flower arrangements on carved chests and ancestral portraits in oil add elegance. Across the hall is the bar and informal dining area decorated with ceiling fans, green glass lamps, and a huge Victorian mirror.

Historic and beautiful, Winona offers excellent recreation. Rich in game fish, the Mississippi's waters may be fished from a sandbar or chartered boat. Scenic cruises of the backwaters reward bird- and animal-watchers, and the river bluffs are laced with

trails. The last wood-hulled stern-wheel steamboat is dry docked on the riverbank and is open to the public, as is the Bunnell House, home of the region's first permanent settler and a fine example of "steamboat gothic."

Mark Twain would be even more enchanted today!

Left. The graceful brass chandeliers are the conversation piece of Zach's dining room. OVERLEAF. At left, natural light bathes the stairway's oak banister, decorative theater scrim, and old-time organ; right, a softly elegant Victorian suite.

THE HOTEL, 129 W. 3rd St., Winona, Minn. 55987; (507) 452-5460; Meta Weiss, Manager. An 1890s hotel, completely renovated. Open all year. Twenty-five rooms with private baths and showers; most with tubs and showers. Rooms tastefully decorated with Victorian-style furniture; all have color TV and telephones. Rates $20 to $40 single; $25 to $60 double. Children under 12, no charge unless special bedding required. Write for year-round special package rates. Zach's Restaurant in hotel serves breakfast, lunch, and dinner. Closed Memorial Day and Christmas Day. Bar lounge and informal dining area popular with public. No pets. MasterCard and Visa credit cards accepted. Golf course, tennis courts, and riding clubs nearby. Children's playground; memorial rose garden on river. Three colleges have programs of theater, concerts, and films. In winter, ice skating, cross-country skiing.

DIRECTIONS: From Minneapolis/St. Paul, take U.S.-61 south to Winona. From Rochester, take U.S.-14 east to Winona.

ANDERSON HOUSE

Wabasha — MINNESOTA

Victorian traditions ... country inn style

When Ida and William Anderson moved from Pennsylvania's Bucks County to the spectacular Mississippi River valley, they brought with them a tradition of Pennsylvania Dutch hospitality. Ida ran the hotel while William worked in the lumber business. Since its opening day in 1856, the hotel doors have never been closed, and much of the original furniture and fixtures are still in use.

Ida Anderson was a superb cook who especially prided herself on the variety and quality of her breads. Today her pride is carried on by granddaughter Ann McCaffrey, who bakes such delicacies as apple nut, prune, dill, tomato, lemon, or apricot kuchen and German rye and Anderson House rolls. Great-grandson John Hall, chef and manager along with mother Jeanne, oversees all other cooking. Waitresses in traditional Dutch costume serve such house specialties as sticky buns, Grandma Anderson's Dutch dumplings, cheese and beer soup, and double Dutch fudge pie. In winter, when the inn is full of skiers, guests might be served scrapple and fastnachts, the breakfast meat dish and plump doughnuts familiar in Pennsylvania's Amish country. In addition to the regular dining room, Ida's Old Fashioned Ice Cream Parlor serves delectable sandwiches and ice creams.

Ida's Victorian antiques furnish the guests rooms on the upper floors of the rambling brick building, now a National Historic Landmark. All rooms are decorated with colorful wallpapers and matching quilted spreads. Suites include a sitting room with TV, private bath, and ornate antique bed.

Pennsylvania Dutch hospitality extends to hot bricks to warm cold beds, mustard plasters for congested chests, shined shoes outside the door if set out the night before, and a choice of six amiable house cats for a bedside companion.

Wabasha is a simple river town, blessed with scenic surroundings, and visitors to the Mayo Clinic in nearby Rochester often make the Anderson their temporary home. Each season brings fresh delights—in spring, guided canoe trips and orchards where you may pick your own fruit; in winter, sleigh rides and cross-country skiing.

At the Anderson the pace is slow, but the care is great!

Upstairs, bedrooms are rainbow-hued. Downstairs, the "no smoking" dining room, *left*, is from another era.

THE ANDERSON HOUSE, 333 Main St., Wabasha, Minn. 55981; (612) 565-4834; John Hall and Jeanne Hall, Innkeepers. A big sprawling small-town hotel on the Mississippi. Open all year. Fifty-two guest rooms, including 5 suites. Private and shared baths. In summer 5 youth hostel rooms share bath; no charge for foreign visitors. Rates, not including meals, $26.50 to $32.50 double, with bath; $18.50 to $24.50 double, without bath. Suites $35, $45. Write for special year-round package rates, including meals. Dining room serves 3 meals a day in summer; closed weekdays for dinner Jan. through March. Closed Thanksgiving and Christmas Day. Ice Cream Parlor open 11AM to 8PM. Children welcome; pets allowed in some rooms. MasterCard, Visa, and Diners Club credit cards accepted. Canoe trips, fishing, tennis, magnificent golf course, 3 miles to Wabasha Historical Society restorations, Lake Pepin, sleigh rides, skiing nearby.

DIRECTIONS: From Minneapolis/St. Paul, take U.S.-61 to Wabasha. At Rte. 60 turn left and drive approximately 1½ miles to Main St. Turn left 3 blocks to hotel. From Rochester, take Rte. 63 to U.S.-61; turn right to Wabasha.

SCHUMACHER'S NEW PRAGUE

New Prague — MINNESOTA

Expect the unexpected in food and decor

Romantic is the key word to describe this unique hotel, a decorating tour de force where old-world charm and sumptuous cuisine combine to ensure warm memories.

Innkeepers John and Nancy Schumacher discovered New Prague and this charming hotel in 1974. Appreciating the elegance and beauty of the building, designed by noted architect Cass Gilbert, they began an extensive renovation and decoration that still continues, although to a visitor all seems perfection.

The Schumachers are representative of a younger generation of innkeepers who gain great satisfaction from running a country inn with all the art and skill they can bring to their pleasurable task. The couple enjoys a creative partnership: John performs his kitchen legerdemain behind the scenes, while Nancy's talents are visibly expressed in the original decor of this gemlike inn, the glorious result of her buying trip to Germany with Bavarian folk painter Pipka. Each of the twelve guest rooms is named for a month of the year with color schemes and furnishing that reflect the seasons. Imported eiderdown comforters and "nun's cap" pillows immediately catch the eye, and Pipka's joyful painting enlivens chairs, beds, wardrobes, and even floors. Her series of delicate European wildflowers decorate the staircase and complement the imported carpeting in soft rose, green, and blue.

The lobby, with its Persian rugs, leather-and-tapestry-covered divans, and wall chests holding John's collections of lead crystal, has a masculine air. "Big Cally's Bar" sports handpainted glass from Germany incorporated into custom leaded windows and cabinets. The jolly handcarved bar stools were designed by Nancy. Imported Czech and German beers and wines are served, as well as the standard beverages. In the '50s-style coffee shop, local citizens drink coffee and read the daily papers provided by the management.

The menu in the dining rooms changes seasonally and reflects John's German heritage and the Czech influence of the town of New Prague. Emphasis is on

Innkeepers John and Nancy Schumacher and family.

game, veal, sausage, and schnitzels of all sorts. John's veal and Czech sausage are highly recommended. Every morning the Czech baker provides a fresh supply of both rye rolls and kolackys, heavenly light nuggets filled with apricot, prune, or poppyseed filling.

Honored as the first hotel in the United States to be included in the European "Romantik Hotels" guidebook, this idyllic hostel is guaranteed to endear itself to any inn-goer.

SCHUMACHER'S NEW PRAGUE HOTEL, 212 W. Main St., New Prague, Minn. 56071; (612) 758-2133; John and Nancy Schumacher. Innkeepers. An exceptional hotel in a quaint country town. Open all year except Dec. 24, 25, 26. Twelve rooms with private baths; TV on request. Rates $49.50 to $59.50 double occupancy; singles $5 less. Three dining rooms serve 3 meals a day, 7 days a week; 2 menus at lunch and dinner; coffee shop and bar. Write for special weekday package rates including meals. Children welcome but no suitable recreation. No pets; no credit cards. Movie theater nearby; golf, tennis, bicycling, cross-country skiing.

DIRECTIONS: From Minneapolis/St. Paul, 35 miles. Take I-35 south to Rte. 19; go west on 19 to New Prague.

Left. "September's" canopied beds are decorated with Czech folk art. Bed curtains are Austrian linen. OVERLEAF. A sunburst leaded glass door arch, ornate grandfather clock, nineteenth-century etching, and John's cut glass collection flank the lobby wall.

NATIONAL HOUSE

Marshall — MICHIGAN

Hard luck town now a national treasure

Innkeeping came as a surprise to Norman Kinney. "The idea was to do as pure a restoration as possible. We got so wrapped up with the building we weren't realistic about what we were going to end up with. We finally realized we were going to have a business to run." Today he and fellow innkeeper Steve Poole run a fine country inn.

After admiring Elizabeth Kinney's Williamsburg garden, guests enter a room where pierced-tin chandeliers softly light rough-hewn beams, wide floorboards, and a huge brick fireplace with a thirteen-foot single-timber mantelpiece. The cream and coral dining room displays antique tables; plate rail collections of tin kitchenware, and kerosene lamps; and a special carpet woven during the Bicentennial and patterned after a nineteenth-century hooked rug.

A continental breakfast of coffee, homemade breads, and rolls is the only meal served at the National House. Guests are urged to visit Win Schuler's restaurant, another Marshall landmark dating from 1909 and the first in a chain of award-winning restaurants in the state.

The familiar sampler motto, "Cleanliness is next to godliness," could appropriately be framed in the fifteen spotless guest rooms. Each has an antique brass or wood bed covered with fine linen. A few rooms overlook the private "sitting garden"; others enjoy a view of Marshall's classical Brooks Fountain at the center of town.

Marshall is noted for its resilience—a quality much in demand in the years since its beginnings in 1830 when it weathered three major calamities. Destined to become the state capital, the town attracted wealthy Easterners, who built elaborate homes—one of them an intended governor's mansion; but a fickle legislature selected Lansing instead as capital. Marshall was then slated to become a key railroad terminal, an expectation that attracted new industries; but the railroad built its maintenance shops in Jackson, and most of the industries were wiped out by a devastating fire. Finally, Marshall seemed to have it made with "pink pills for pale people." The patent medicine business boomed—until the Pure Food and Drug Act!

But Marshall survived and is one of the best examples of mid-nineteenth-century architecture in America. Marshall was chosen by The National Trust for Historic Preservation for its first meeting outside of Washington. And the wonder of it all is that this restoration and revitalization has been accomplished with private funds.

To fully enjoy a visit to this landmark town, the National House is the place to stay.

Left. The soft-hued shades of the Sidney Ketchum suite contrast with the rough-hewn warmth of the lobby, above. OVERLEAF. Spurred by civic pride, merchants are active in the restoration of Marshall as an architectural showcase.

THE NATIONAL HOUSE INN, 102 S. Parkview, Marshall, Mich. 49068; (616) 781-7374; Norman D. Kinney, Steven W. Poole, Innkeepers. Open all year except Christmas Eve and Christmas Day. Fifteen guest rooms with private baths; some shared showers. Rates $45 to $50 double; singles $3 less. Includes continental breakfast. Children welcome; no pets. MasterCard, Visa credit cards accepted. Guest privileges at tennis and racquet club; golf course; cross-country skiing. Walking and driving tours of city; tree tour; annual Home Tour, weekend after Labor Day; Honolulu House Museum.

DIRECTIONS: From Detroit, take I-94 west to Marshall exit. In town circle right at fountain; inn on southwest corner. From Lansing, take I-69 south to Michigan Ave. Exit 36.

DEARBORN INN

Dearborn — MICHIGAN

America preserved, tradition reborn

The pleasure of exploring Greenfield Village and the Henry Ford Museum, two famous American institutions, is enhanced by a stay at the Dearborn Inn. Henry Ford, the genius behind these three establishments, said of the first two: "When we are through, we shall have reproduced American life as lived." The inn resonates with these words, blending colonial style with contemporary hospitality.

A stately colonial mansion furnished in Early American, the inn boasts a lobby of quiet luxury, with crystal chandeliers, elegant handpainted wallpaper and a portrait of Henry Ford over the fireplace. The comfortable bedrooms are furnished in traditional style.

Behind the inn are reproductions of five colonial homes that belonged to Americans whom Ford admired. Slight alterations have made them suitable as guest accommodations, but many of the furnishings are reproductions of the originals. There is Walt Whitman's birthplace, with handhewn cedar shingles; Edgar Allan Poe's cozy cottage; the stately Patrick Henry house; Barbara Fritchie's modest dwelling, complete with reproduction of the Union flag hanging from her bedroom window; and Governor Oliver Wolcott's Connecticut home.

The Motor House is modern motel living at its finest. Close to its doorstep are a swimming pool, tennis courts, and a children's playground.

In addition to a formal Early American dining room, the Ten Eyck Tavern—named for Conrad "Coon" Ten Eyck, who operated the first wayside inn in Michigan—offers casual dining. In both, American fare is prepared to perfection with the emphasis on fresh, high-quality ingredients and such specialties as broiled fresh whitefish and golden pickerel, Michigan bean soup, chewy salt rolls, Dearborn cheesecake, and Michigan apple pie.

Guests should allow at least two days to explore the 250 acres and 85 historic buildings that make up the Greenfield Village/Henry Ford Museum complex. Among the original structures in the village are the

Left. The inn's lobby, with intricate ceiling medallions, hand-painted onion skin wallpaper, and Oriental rugs, is watched over by Henry Ford.

The Patrick Henry and Oliver Woolcot houses.

Wright brothers' workshop; Edison's Menlo Park laboratory; the Illinois courthouse where Lincoln practiced law; the home where Ford was raised; and Noah Webster's house. You can ride two century-old steam trains and a paddlewheel steamboat, or watch artisans working at old-time crafts. The museum's artifacts record the birth of America's home crafts and show their evolution to heavy industry; you will see the development of the locomotive, of production-line machinery, factory furniture, lighting, household appliances, aircraft, and the automobile. Fascinating Ford memorabilia, including the first car, are also displayed.

A visit to the Dearborn Inn, the Ford Museum, and Greenfield Village proves that Henry was a man of his word.

THE DEARBORN INN, 20301 Oakwood Blvd., Dearborn, Mich. 48123; (313) 271-2700; Adrian de Vogel, General Manager. A handsome inn reflecting the best of our colonial heritage. Open all year. The 180 guest rooms are located in the inn itself, in 5 colonial homes, and in the Motor House. Rates $50.50 to $65 single; $58.72 double; suites $125 to $145. Rollaways $5; cribs no charge. Write for special 1-night weekend rate and for Weekend Vacation. The formal Early American dining room serves lunch and dinner Monday through Friday; Saturday dinner only; Sunday brunch and dinner. Ten Eyck Tavern serves 3 meals every day. A luncheon buffet is served Monday through Friday in the Golden Eagle cocktail lounge. All restaurants are open to public, and food is served 365 days a year. Children welcome; pets accepted. MasterCard, Visa credit cards accepted. Swimming, tennis, visits to Greenfield Village, Henry Ford Museum, and Sunday tours of Ford's home.

DIRECTIONS: From Detroit, take I-94 west to Oakwood north exit. Go 2 miles on Oakwood to inn across from Ford test track. From Chicago, take I-94 east to Oakwood north exit.

Farmington Hills

BOTSFORD INN

MICHIGAN

Henry Ford's favorite inn

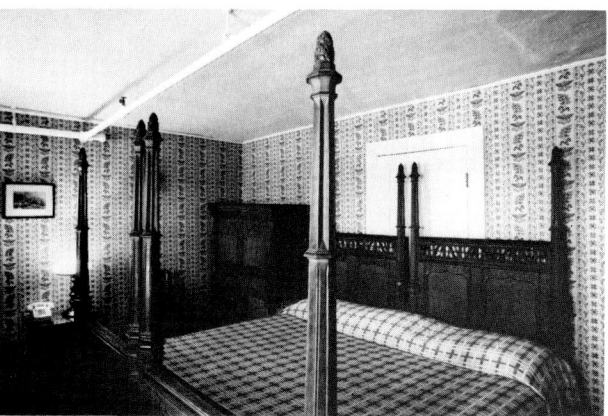
The bedroom set made for Thomas Edison.

A century and a half ago the Botsford Inn was a favorite coach stop on the old Post Road between Detroit and Lansing. Here farmers and drovers met to trade goods and swap stories. In the early 1900s the inn's existence was threatened by impending road improvements. Young Henry Ford, who had met his future wife, Clara, at a square dance at the inn, heard of the Botsford's plight. He bought the inn and, employing heroic measures, moved it 300 feet to safety. He then began a painstaking restoration that ignored no detail. After paneling one of the dining rooms, for example, he filled its fireplace with corncobs, set them ablaze, and sealed the room, a curing method he had seen used on his Georgia plantation. The result was a mellow antique finish.

Ford kept the inn, operating it as a rather eccentric tearoom until his death in 1947. Four years later, present innkeeper John Anhut bought it and added treasured furnishings from Henry and Clara's estate. In the living room may be seen Henry's pet, a Swiss Stella music box, complete with perforated metal playing discs and encased in ornately carved mahogany. Clara's pianochord dates from 1801, and there is also a fine inlaid rosewood table with a case of Henry's beloved knickknacks. In one guest room is a Gothic bedroom set of handcarved fumed oak, made for Thomas Edison's bedroom at the Ford home.

With the addition of two modern wings, the inn now has sixty-five guest accommodations. Sensitive to the needs of his guests, John Anhut says: "One of my fetishes is to have movable reading lamps in each room, and another is to provide full-length mirrors throughout." Other amenities include air conditioning, color TV, AM/FM clock-radios, and complimentary coffee.

Beautiful grounds enhance the inn and protect it from the encroachment of the city. Diners in the newest of the Botsford's six dining rooms look out through floor-to-ceiling windows on a walled lawn and garden, and forget they are only a few miles from the heart of town.

Fine food and service attract a loyal following. The inn specializes in Early American fare, including beef short ribs, Dutch oven chicken, roast turkey, johnny cakes, and eggnog pie.

Open to wayfarers since 1836, this "oldest operating inn in the state of Michigan" offers the best of the country in the city.

Left. Model of the U.S.S. *Constitution.*

THE BOTSFORD INN, 2800 Grand River Rd., Farmington Hills, Mich. 48024; (313) 474-4800; John W. Anhut, Innkeeper. A handsome, white frame inn with two-story porches. Open all year. Sixty-five guest rooms with private baths. Rates $30 to $40 single; $35 to $50 double; suites $50 up. Six dining rooms serving 3 meals a day open to public. Closed Mondays, Memorial Day, Christmas Day, New Year's Day. Coffee available Mondays for overnight guests. Children welcome; pets not encouraged. MasterCard, Visa, American Express credit cards accepted. Swimming pool; patio for card playing; 35 minutes by expressway to Renaissance Center in downtown Detroit.

DIRECTIONS: From Detroit, take I-75 north to 8 Mile Rd. (Rte. 102). Go west on 8 Mile Rd. to Grand River Rd.; turn right on Grand River to inn. From Chicago, take I-94 east to I-275 north. Stay on 275 to Rte. 102, 8 Mile Rd. Go east to Grand River Rd.; turn left to inn.

ST. CLAIR INN

St. Clair — MICHIGAN

A riverside haven for weary travelers

Freighters gliding soundlessly by this large, handsome Tudor-style inn invite the guest to gaze, relax and enjoy. "The Inn on the River" is a landmark to local citizens. Originally built in 1926 as a community center and a stopover for that burgeoning breed called "tourists," it is now much enlarged and offers good food, friendly surroundings, and a spectacular vantage point from which to view the parade of ships. In winter the lobby with its blazing fires is a cozy spot for watching giant ice floes.

A quarter-mile walk to town on the river boardwalk or a dip in the indoor pool sharpens the appetite. Diners may be tempted to try shark amandine, or perhaps the more traditional St. Clair River pickerel, on the daily menu since the inn opened.

Though only forty-nine miles from busy Detroit, the inn is far enough off the beaten track to combine charm with unhurried personal service.

ST. CLAIR INN, 500 N. Riverside Ave., St. Clair, Mich. 48079; (313) 329-2222, toll-free WATS line 1-800-482-8327; Mike La Porte, Innkeeper. Though large enough to provide facilities for business conferences, there is sufficient intimacy to appeal to individuals and couples. Open all year. More than 70 guest rooms with private baths, TV, radio, air conditioning. All rates based on double occupancy. Inn proper $34 to $44; suite $152. River Station suites $62 to $137. Captain's House 3-bedroom suite $202; motel type annex $42 to $54.50. Write for group rates with meals. Breakfast, lunch, and dinner served in several dining rooms open to public. Closed Christmas Day. Children welcome; no pets. MasterCard, Visa, American Express credit cards accepted. Country Club privileges for guests: 2 18-hole golf courses, tennis, racquetball; municipal marina for boating; transportation provided for golfers, shoppers.

DIRECTIONS: From Detroit, take I-94 east to St. Clair exit; turn right for 6 miles. At flashing light turn right to traffic signal and left to inn. From Port Huron, take Rte. 29 south to St. Clair. Inn on Rte. 29. St. Clair airport 8 miles from inn.

Mackinac Island # WINDERMERE HOTEL
MICHIGAN

A hotel like the summer homes of your childhood

Since 1904 the Doud family has owned and operated the Windermere, a large, handsome yellow frame "cottage," once a magnificent summer house and now home for many visitors to this enchanting island. The views of the quaint harbor and the sparkling waters of the Straits of Mackinac from its wide verandas and comfortable guest rooms are stunning.

The history of the island is alive in the person of innkeeper Robert Doud. His grandparents came to the island in the 1850s in flight from Ireland's potato famine and set up business as coopers. Uncle Patrick Doud was a contractor who operated the Windermere until his retirement. Robert, who ran the Doud grocery, took it over more than thirty-five years ago. Today he manages the hotel with daughter Margaret, who also is serving a term as town mayor.

A stay at the Windermere would not be complete without a visit to Windermere Imports, just down the street.

WINDERMERE HOTEL, Mackinac Island, Mich. 49757; (906) 847-3301 or 3491; Robert V. Doud and Margaret M. Doud, Innkeepers. Hospitality has been dispensed at the Windermere for more than 75 years. Open May 20 through end of Oct. Rates for the comfortable guest rooms, all with private baths and many with stunning views, $55 to $66 single or double occupancy. No meals are served but the town abounds with a variety of restaurants. Children welcome; cribs, rollaways available. No pets. MasterCard, Visa credit cards accepted. Cards and board games in hotel; Windermere Point Park across street; swimming, golf, tennis, bicycling, hiking, riding, island tours, sailboat rentals, charter fishing.

DIRECTIONS: From lower peninsula, take I-75 north to Mackinaw City; ferries leave every ½ hour during season, less frequently off-season. From upper peninsula, take I-75 south to St. Ignace. Same ferry schedule. Once off ferry turn left; hotel is at west end of Main St.

HOTEL IROQUOIS

Mackinac Island — MICHIGAN

A fine old island hotel delightfully redecorated

Foghorn on a misty morning, seagulls' cries by day, and taps sounding from the fort at nightfall set the mood for a vacation on this very special island. The Hotel Iroquois, owned and run for twenty-eight years by innkeepers Margaret and Sam McIntyre is the ideal vacation home. Built at the water's edge in 1902, it needed work when the McIntyres took over. "In the beginning, we had no money for redecoration, but we made up for it by keeping the place very clean." This cleanliness remains the inn's hallmark and, together with service, the basis of its success. Every guest receives prompt, cheerful attention from the staff.

From small cozy rooms overlooking Main Street to deluxe suites with window alcoves jutting out over the shore, each of the forty-eight rooms has a view of the water; and each is individually decorated with pleasing floral wallpaper, soft carpeting, and reading lamps.

The Iroquois has a deserved reputation for the best food in town. A continental breakfast of orange juice, fresh-baked blueberry muffins, and coffee is available in guests' rooms. Lunch features soup, salad, and a variety of sandwiches, the most popular being the grilled crab, lobster, and shrimp combination. At dinner the menu offers Lake Superior whitefish—an island specialty—center-cut pork chops, fried chicken, filet mignon, veal cutlets, and a daily special. There is a small but well-chosen wine list, and among the homemade desserts the famous Mackinac Island Fudge Ice Cream Puff is an instant sellout.

Left. Margaret McIntyre's deft touch is expressed in the decor of each guest room.

Sightseeing is a popular pastime and easily accomplished on this island of only 8.2 miles in circumference. Because of Mackinac's ban on automobiles, horse-drawn carriages serve every transportation need. Guests may rent drive-it-yourself carriages. Bicycling and hiking on the many well-marked scenic trails are popular recreations. At Fort Mackinac, built by the British during the Revolution, one can trace the history of the island from the time when Indians farmed it through the period from 1780 to 1835 when it was the center of the fur trade. In 1810 John Jacob Astor laid the foundation here of his immense fortune with the American Fur Company.

Mackinac is rewarding for both children and grown-ups. In 1836 a visiting Englishwoman proclaimed the island to be "the wildest and tenderest little piece of beauty" she had ever seen. It still is.

HOTEL IROQUOIS ON THE BEACH, Mackinac Island (pronounced Mackinaw), Mich. 49757; (906) 847-3321; Sam and Margaret McIntyre, Innkeepers. A 48-room white frame hotel on the water's edge at Windermere Pt. Private baths. Open early May to late Oct. Continental breakfast during summer season at extra charge. Full breakfast available at nearby restaurants. Hotel restaurant, open to public, serves complete lunch and dinner during summer season. Rates June 15 to Sept. 24, $58 to $104, double occupancy; deluxe suites $114. $100 deposit requested for each room reserved. Rates do not include meals. Children welcome; no pets. MasterCard and Visa credit cards accepted. Swimming at private beach or public pool; golf courses, tennis courts, bicycling, hiking, horseback riding, island tours, sailboat rentals, charter fishing.

DIRECTIONS: From lower peninsula, take I-75 north to Mackinaw City; ferries leave every half-hour during season, less frequently off-season. From upper peninsula, take I-75 south to St. Ignace. Same ferry schedule as from Mackinaw City. By air, Republic Airways to Pellston, Mich.; limousine to Mackinaw City. Charter plane service from Pellston Airport to island airstrip.

Bay View # STAFFORD'S BAY VIEW MICHIGAN

Where a great innkeeper runs a great inn

A stellar presence in northern Michigan's famed vacation area, Stafford's Bay View Inn has all the charm of the classic resort: cool breezes off the bay, a wealth of outdoor recreation, a variety of cultural events, and the perfect ambience for drowsing over a book. Stafford's offers the vacationer an idyllic existence.

Situated in the tiny village of Bay View, a stone's throw from bustling Petoskey, Stafford's enjoys the best of both worlds. Bay View was established in 1875 as a Methodist campground "for intellectual and scientific culture and the promotion of the cause of religion and morality." The prevailing atmosphere is peaceful; the speed limit is 20 mph; and the Methodists still present excellent concerts, lectures, and religious services. Petoskey, on the other hand, is a shopper's mecca, with its picturesque Gaslight District as the northern outpost for many art galleries and chic Palm Beach boutiques.

Searching for Petoskey stones is another popular pastime. These are fossil corals that lived in salty warm water 300 millions years ago. Today they are found along the shores of Little Traverse Bay and, when polished, reveal beautiful star burst clusters of soft dove gray.

When Stafford Smith bought his turn-of-the-century inn, it needed extensive repair. He and his wife, Janice, have refurnished it, preserving the old-fashioned feeling of the original clapboard house. It is hard to imagine a cozier spot; its comfortable accommodations, good food, and friendly atmosphere are legendary. Duncan Hines included the Bay View

Searching for Petoskey stones is a must.

in his popular books for travelers, *Adventures in Good Eating*, and the inn still specializes in excellent home cooking. Especially popular are the Friday night fish buffet with soup and salad bar, Saturday's "good neighbor" roast lamb and beef buffet, and a trencherman's Sunday brunch. There is no bar, but drinks will be served to overnight guests who provide their own spirits.

Having established a reputation for fine food, Stafford opened another restaurant in neighboring Harbor Springs. Once a boathouse, The Pier offers a panoramic view of the waterfront, a continental menu, a generous cheese and salad bar, and cocktails in the Wheelhouse Lounge.

Guests feel especially at ease at the Bay View Inn, and it is no mystery why. Innkeeper nonpareil, Stafford Smith's warm personality, good humor, and an almost prescient ability to foresee a guests's needs make the Bay View a traveler's haven.

Each guest room is highly individual.

STAFFORD'S BAY VIEW INN, Box 3, Petoskey, Mich. 49770; (616) 347-2771; Stafford Smith, Innkeeper and Owner; Kathy Hart, Manager. Distinctive Victorian cottage with mansard roof. Opening and closing dates flexible, usually from May 25 through Labor Day. Closed April, May, Nov. Twenty-two rooms with private baths. Summer rates $29 to $39 per person, double occupancy; $20 single. Winter weekend $50 to $65 for 2 nights including 3 meals. Dining room open to public for 3 meals a day. Children welcome; small pets accepted. Indoor tennis, racquetball nearby; boating, fishing, downhill skiing nearby; ice boating, skating, snowmobiling.

DIRECTIONS: From southern Michigan, take I-75 to Gaylord exit to Rte. 32. Turn left on 32 and go 13 miles to junction with U.S.-131. Go north 21 miles on 131 to Petoskey. Inn is 1 mile beyond city limits. From northern Michigan, take I-75 south to Indian River exit. Turn right onto Rte. 68. Go 11 miles to Alanson, then south on U.S.-31 to Bay View.

BIRCHWOOD INN

Harbor Springs — MICHIGAN

Motel with a luxurious difference

"A damn good little motel," is how innkeeper Earl Larson describes Birchwood Inn. But though this series of long low buildings may *look* like a motel, the resemblance ends there.

Earl, ever attentive, brews fresh coffee early in the morning and arranges the fresh-baked pastries. You may breakfast on the lawn—with its colorful umbrellas, potted geraniums, and horses grazing in a nearby pasture—or, if the weather is crisp, in front of a blazing fire in the cheery Lodge Fireside room, where relaxation settles over you like a warm blanket.

The Arboretum next door, a softly lit restaurant with fresh flowers and exotic birds, serves delicious and inventive food. Dinner might be "Steak 17"—sliced sirloin topped with red onions and mushrooms sautéed in sherry and drawn butter—or the quail and perch combo; and conclude with a "Dirt Ball," just one of the mind-boggling chocolate desserts!

BIRCHWOOD INN, Lake Shore Dr., Harbor Springs, Mich. 49740; (616) 526-2151; Earl and Sally Larson, Innkeepers. A low, rambling inn overlooking rolling hills, with Traverse Bay beyond. Forty-four spacious guest rooms with private baths. Open all year except from mid-March to April 1. After Jan. 3, open Thursday through Monday night only. Rates $28 single, except July and Aug. when no single guests accepted. Double occupancy $39 to $55. Rates include continental breakfast. Inn has no restaurant, but the Arboretum next door is open to the public for dinner. Children welcome; no pets. MasterCard, Visa credit cards accepted. Heated swimming pool, tennis courts, shuffleboard. Inn affiliated with 2 magnificent private golf courses. Public beach in Harbor Springs. Bird and deer hunting nearby; noted ski area nearby. Elegant summer shops in Harbor Springs and Petoskey.

DIRECTIONS: From southern Michigan, take I-75 north to Gaylord exit. Go west on Rte. 32 approximately 10 miles to U.S.-131. Go north on 131 to intersection of Rte. 119. Go approximately 8 miles to Harbor Springs. Inn on 119, 2 miles past Harbor Springs.

Left. The inn's lounge is a place where guests enjoy gathering. *Below.* An idyllic corner of the inn's grounds.

Poynette # JAMIESON HOUSE   WISCONSIN

Hugh Sr.'s manse, which houses the dining rooms.

Dine well, sleep well in two elegant mansions

In 1970 Hugh Jamieson's century-old mansion was a near ruin. It had been forty-three years since it was last occupied, and the house was slated for demolition when Jeff and June Smith visited it and felt compelled to restore it to the grandeur achieved by Jamieson, a successful grain and lumber merchant and civic leader. Restoration was a tremendous job; the entire interior had to be dismantled, but the original grained woodwork was carefully removed, refinished, and replaced. To skeptics who shook their heads over the magnitude of the task, the Smiths proclaimed it "an exciting labor of love" and hoped that their guests would "feel the same warmth of hospitality that the home's owners exuded a century ago."

Besides being inveterate travelers, the Smiths both loved to entertain. Also, Jeff says, "We were interested in the pursuit of excellence, which is difficult to achieve if you're working for someone else." With this ambition, they set out to open a fine restaurant, incorporating in their menu many exotic dishes discovered in their travels. Today the restaurant offers a seven-course, prix fixe dinner, featuring such specialties as filet of beef with blue cheese sauce, chicken breasts with toasted hazelnut sauce, and curried lamb with walnut and lemon. Each dinner includes an aperitif, soup and hors d'oeuvres, salad, homemade rolls, and a choice of vegetables. Dessert, served in the Garden Room, might include a delectable lemon mousse made from lemons growing on a tree in the corner.

With June retired from the business, Jeff is responsible for the preparatory cooking and baking but still finds time to conduct seminars and classes in cooking.

In time, Jeff bought the house across the street, built in 1883 by Hugh Jamieson's eldest son. While smaller than the main house, it is equally elegant and is now a luxurious four-bedroom guest house. The master suite is stylishly furnished with Victorian pieces and has a bathroom with a curtained six-foot tub and floor-to-ceiling mirrors. The drawing room contains the cedar chest Hugh, Jr., took to college and horsehair chairs from the original mansion. The house's only drawback for some is a no-smoking rule.

JAMIESON HOUSE, 407 N. Franklin, Poynette, Wis. 53955; (608) 635-4100; Jeffrey Smith, Innkeeper. Two elegantly restored Victorian mansions, one a restaurant, the other, across the street, a guest house. Open all year. Four guest accommodations with private baths. $45 for rooms, $55 for suites. No smoking in guest house. Restaurant, comprising several small, elegantly decorated dining rooms, serves 7-course prix fixe dinner only, 7 days a week to overnight guests; Wednesday through Sunday open to public. Extensive wine list. Closed Christmas Eve, Christmas Day, and New Year's Day. Children welcome; well-behaved pets accepted. No credit cards. Recreation activities at McKenzie Environmental Center, 1 mile from town, a nature park with birds, Wisconsin wild animals, plants, trees, picnic area. Horse farm 1 mile from town with riding and trails. Six miles from Lake Wisconsin with fishing, boating. Antique and art shops in neighborhood. Inn will pack picnic lunch.

DIRECTIONS: From Milwaukee, take I-90, 94 to Country Road CS east to Poynette. Follow for 3 miles to Main St. Go north through town, turn right on Hudson. Inn on corner of Franklin.

Left. Each dining table is set with Bavarian china and sterling silver. In the luxurious red dining room beyond, Jeff's collection of cranberry glass is displayed. OVERLEAF. The Garden Room, where dessert is served.

OLD RITTENHOUSE INN

Bayfield — WISCONSIN

Victorian opulence on Lake Superior

If it is possible for an inn to be *too* beautiful, the Old Rittenhouse wins the title. From its flower-filled veranda with comfortable wicker furniture, to the exquisitely appointed dining rooms and elegant guest rooms, one is struck, time and again, by the inn's opulence. Dedicated collectors, skilled restorers, and talented decorators, Mary and Jerry Phillips have created a heady environment that expresses their complex and gifted personalities.

The Phillipses, who met at the University of Wisconsin Graduate School of Music, first exercised their knack for preservation by restoring a condemned house in Madison. Spotting a For Sale sign on a turn-of-the-century Victorian mansion in Bayfield, they peeked in the windows and promptly made a down payment. After ongoing restoration and two years of running the house as a summertime bed-and-breakfast, they moved to Bayfield permanently in 1975, and the Old Rittenhouse became a full-fledged inn.

In addition to a stunning collection of Victorian lamps—including a signed Tiffany—the inn is furnished with a treasure trove of china, silver, crystal, and antiques of all kinds. The Phillipses' collections represent past investments and an exhaustive search for "just the right things."

The five guest rooms differ in character but not in comfort. The largest contains a king-size bed dressed in white eyelet and ruffles, a cranberry glass chandelier, and an ornate marble-topped vanity. Fireplaces in most of the guest rooms provide welcome heat in crisp weather.

Dining at the inn is a special event. Jerry, tuxedo clad, greets the diners and lights the table's single taper. Recitation of the menu in his trained voice is spellbinding.

In the kitchen Mary gives her own private concert— a nightly tour de force that might include fresh trout poached in champagne, steak Bercy stuffed with oysters, curried scallops, or a hearty pork ragout. All meals begin with soup and salad, and fresh homemade breads are served steaming hot and in endless supply.

At dessert time Jerry reappears. Only the most dedicated dieter could resist a rich sundae after the toppings have been so sensuously described.

By day, guests can explore Bayfield, now on the National Register of Historic Places, and the Apostle Islands just off the shore of Lake Superior. The area is a spectacular setting for an inn that does it full justice.

Above and OVERLEAF *at left. Victorian lamps of all kinds are a hallmark of the inn, and right, the sunny veranda is scented with spicy petunias. The following photograph is of beautiful Bayfield, now on the National Register of Historic Places.*

OLD RITTENHOUSE INN, Bayfield, Wis. 54814; (715) 779-5765; Jerry and Mary Phillips, Innkeepers. Sumptuous hilltop Victorian mansion, decorated with fine antiques. Open all year except Nov. and Jan. Dining room closed Christmas Day. Five guest rooms with private and shared baths. Breakfast is served only for overnight guests. Double occupancy rates $50 with private bath and fireplace; $30 with shared bath. Children not encouraged; no pets. No credit cards. Dining room open to public by reservation. While there is no nightlife in Bayfield, by day it offers a wide choice of recreation: fishing, sailing, cruising Lake Superior's Apostle Islands National Lakeshore, scenic drives, visits to Madeleine Island State Park, berry picking in season, canoeing on Brule River. In summer Bayfield hosts a number of fairs including the Tri-State Arts and Crafts Fair on the waterfront. Cross-country skiing in winter.

DIRECTIONS: From Minneapolis/St. Paul, take U.S.-94 east to Rte. 63. Follow Rte. 63 north to Rte. 2. Go east 8 miles to Rte. 13 north to Bayfield. Inn is on Rte. 13 on corner of Rittenhouse Ave. and 3rd St. From Duluth, take U.S.-2 east 60 miles to Rte. 13 at Ashland. Follow Rte. 13 north to Bayfield. From Ironwood, take U.S.-2 west 40 miles to Rte. 13.

BAY SHORE INN

Sturgeon Bay — WISCONSIN

A complete summer resort at one spectacular inn

The sun-drenched lawn, filled with flowers and gnarled relics of an apple orchard, sweeps to the beach. You have arrived at the Bay Shore Inn on Sturgeon Bay.

It all began in 1921 when John and Matilda Hanson converted their barn into a guest house and kitchen. The Hansons had farmed their land for more than three decades, and during those years more and more city folks discovered the charms of Door County. In time Matilda's cooking became renowned. Her butter-fried chicken and Door County cherry pie were legendary. Garden and orchard produce provisioned the kitchen, just as they do today. Duke Hanson, Matilda's son, tends the large garden and harvests the fruits and vegetables that feature prominently in the Bay Shore Inn's famous cuisine. Chef and manager Paul Mathias has added some sophisticated touches to the menu while preserving the spirit of Matilda Hanson's cooking.

The Bay Shore Inn is tailored to families. All meals and recreational facilities are included in the price of a visit. The inn consists of various accommodations; a rustic main lodge, A-frame chalets, beach and ranch terrace units, and Early American cottages. All guest rooms have private baths and TV.

The choice of recreation at Bay Shore is amazingly large and varied. Swimming and water skiing are popular since the waters of Sturgeon Bay are warmer than those of the adjoining Green Bay and Lake Michigan. Guests may learn to sail the sporty but safe sailfish or go out in the inn's big sloop, a Pearson Ensign day sailer. Tours of Sturgeon Bay shipyards and Green Bay are conducted in the *Duchess II* a large motor cruiser. Athletes can row across the bay to the magnificent Potowatomie State Park. For children there is a slide, a raft, and a special dock in

Duke Hanson shows off his fall harvest.

shallow waters. Fishing is a major activity; and among land sports are tennis, archery, badminton, croquet, and horseshoes. Shuffleboard and a variety of indoor games may be enjoyed in the recreation building. Riding stables and five golf courses are nearby.

Reservations are essential at this carefree, self-contained resort, where guests return year after year.

BAY SHORE INN, 4205 Bay Shore Dr., Sturgeon Bay, Wis. 54235; (414) 743-4551; the Hansons and Mathiases, Innkeepers. A large family-oriented inn with full resort facilities and wide range of accommodations. Open mid-May to late Oct. Rates July 1 to Sept. 1, $43 to $49 per person with breakfast and dinner. Optional basket lunch or beach barbecue. Without meals, $30 to $36 per person. Dining room open to inn guests only. Write for off-season, weekend, and weekly rates, and description of accommodations. Children welcome; no pets. No credit cards. Full range of outdoor sports. Indoor games in large recreation room with fireplace.

DIRECTIONS: From Green Bay, Wis., take Rte. 57 to Business, cross bridge and turn left on N. 1st Ave.; go past shipyards to 3rd. Turn left on 3rd and drive approximately 3 miles to inn on left.

Left. The fireplace in the rustic main lodge is faithfully tended when the weather is crisp.

Fish Creek — WISCONSIN

WHITE GULL INN

The fish boil dinner highlights your stay

"The White Gull does not put on airs," asserts innkeeper Andy Coulson. Indeed, the first impulse on arrival at this turn-of-the-century white clapboard inn is to rummage in the suitcase for comfortable clothes.

Innkeepers Jan and Andy Coulson and their youthful staff maintain the casual atmosphere, and the inn's guest rooms range from antique-filled to purely utilitarian. In addition to rooms in the inn, separate cottages are particularly suited to families and small groups. The dining room serves three meals a day to guests and the public. The exciting event is the famous White Gull fish boil, served rain or shine on Wednesday, Friday, Saturday, and Sunday nights. Reservations are essential for this dinner that draws the hungry and eager from all over the peninsula.

Master boiler Russ Ostrand enlivens the ritual with tunes from a tiny accordion as he presides on the patio. A giant cauldron of boiling water over a beechwood fire quickly cooks a batch of red-skinned potatoes. Then an openwork basket filled with whitefish steaks is lowered into the boiling water, resting there precisely eight minutes. The climactic moment comes when Russ tosses kerosene on the fire. Instantly, ten-foot flames lick the sky while onlookers retreat. The water boils over, flushing any impurities from the pot. The fish is rushed inside and served with melted butter, fresh coleslaw, homemade breads, and Door County cherry pie. Legions of enthusiastic diners swear no finer fish dinner exists.

On Monday and Thursday nights in summer and fall, an early American buffet is served. Guests choose from such old-fashioned goodies as turkey dumpling soup, glazed baked ham, corn and clam pie, maple-glazed carrots, Boston baked beans, scalloped potatoes, and an assortment of salads and desserts. Serving begins at 6PM and reservations are advised.

Door County is a place to explore, and Fish Creek is an excellent starting point, offering clear water, sandy beaches, and a sheltered cove for fishing. Peninsula State Park, Wisconsin's most beautiful, begins here. Thousands of acres of virgin forest, ma-

jestic cliffs, caves, and rugged coastline invite the visitor.

Unique in Fish Creek are the Peninsula Players, America's oldest professional summer stock company, which performs from July through Labor Day. The Peninsula Music Festival in August is a happy gathering of musicians from famous orchestras across the country.

Left. At a fish boil, the climax comes when kerosene is tossed on the flames, boiling off the impurities on the top of the brew.

THE WHITE GULL INN, Box 175, Fish Creek, Wis. 54212; (414) 868-3517; Andy and Jan Coulson, Innkeepers; Joan Holliday, Manager. An informal inn on Wisconsin's Green Bay. Open early May to Oct. 26; Dec. 26 to mid-March. Nine lodge rooms with private and shared baths. Rates $25 to $30; weekly rate 10% off daily rate. Cottages with bath and TV, 4 persons $50, $255 weekly; 5 persons $55, $275 weekly; 6 persons $60, $295 weekly. Without bath, $25. Housekeeping cottage, up to 4 persons $225 per week, minimum stay. Dining room, serving 3 meals a day, open to public. Children welcome; small pets in cottages only. No credit cards. Swimming, fishing, bicycling, jogging on 1½-mile exclusive road, 18-hole golf course, roller skating, hiking, sailboat rentals.

DIRECTIONS: From Green Bay, Wis., take Rte. 57 north through Sturgeon Bay to Sister Bay where it becomes Rte. 42. Continue to Fish Creek. Inn on Main St.

Ellison Bay   # GRIFFIN INN   WISCONSIN

Corporate careers succumb to innkeeping

For Joyce and Paul Crittenden, the Griffin Inn is what dreams are made of. Early in 1979 they evaluated their priorities. "When we drew up separate lists, and work wasn't on either of them, it made us stop and think," explained Joyce. "We had had it with the whole corporate structure." By May the Crittendens had given up lucrative careers in Milwaukee for the round-the-clock demands of innkeeping. Two qualities combined to ensure success: the Crittendens' twenty-four years of collective professional experience and deep-felt satisfaction with their new independence.

After weeks of cleaning, restoring, and furnishing their old-fashioned frame guest house, they opened their first season. The inn quickly acquired a reputation for high standards and a loyal following. To maintain these standards, the Crittendens do everything themselves, from cleaning and laundering to apple picking in their own orchard. Joyce, a talented and creative cook, rises at six each morning to bake bread and prepare breakfast. This satisfying meal includes either a soufflé, quiche, or omelet; potatoes or hot cereal; fresh-baked rolls or muffins; and coffeecake or pancakes for dessert. During the winter season, rates include three meals a day. The dinner menu features such delicacies as a seafood mousse appetizer, cream of peanut or sauerkraut soup, and crabcakes with caper sauce, served along with a garden salad and Indian pudding or apple fritters for dessert.

Ten second-floor guest rooms share one-and-a-half baths. Rooms are furnished with antique beds and chests and rainbow-hued quilts. Two rustic wood-paneled cabins with four separate units nestle behind the house. Hiking, running, or just strolling is popular in the Clearing, a lovely wooded area marked with miles of smooth, tree-shaded trails. In winter this is cross-country skiing territory and skis may be rented at the inn. A platter of just-warm-from-the-oven molasses bars often awaits the skiers' return. Throughout the year the living room with its fireplace is the focus of activity, be it no more than sharing good company and the nightly bowl of fresh popcorn.

Left. A corner of the sitting room illustrates the homey, unpretentious furnishings of this lakeside inn.

A real antique and still going strong.

The Griffin Inn is a superb example of a dream come true.

GRIFFIN INN, 1 Mink River Rd., Ellison Bay, Wis. 54210; (414) 854-4306; Joyce and Paul Crittenden, Innkeepers. This New England-style white clapboard inn is open all year except April and Nov. Ten rooms in main house share 1½ baths. Two cabins have 2 double units, each with toilet and shower. Rates in inn April through Oct., $29 single; $35 double; $42 triple, including full breakfast. Cabins $30 double not including breakfast; each additional person $4.50. Weekly rates in cabins 10% off daily rates. Does not include daily maid service. Winter rates, Nov. through March, $65 double, including 3 meals. Write for special packages. Dining room open to inn guests only. Children welcome in cabins; no pets. No credit cards. Volleyball, horseshoes on grounds; bikes and skis to rent; golf, riding, tennis, cross-country skiing, museums, swimming, potters, antique shops, and restaurants all short walk or drive from inn.

DIRECTIONS: From Green Bay, Wis., take Rte. 57 north through Sturgeon Bay to Sister Bay where it becomes Rte. 42. Continue to Ellison Bay; turn right just before information center. Look for inn sign about ½ mile before turn. Go two blocks to inn on left.

HOTEL DU NORD

Sister Bay — WISCONSIN

A rustic lodge on Wisconsin's fabled peninsula

"We always try to keep quality consistently high," says innkeeper Keyes Fletcher. The Hotel du Nord is noted for some of the best food in Door County, prepared by two chefs and a baker. Popular entrées include chicken pan-fried in butter, broiled shrimp wrapped in bacon and served on a bed of wild rice pilaff, and fresh-caught Lake Michigan whitefish and perch. Dinner rolls and desserts—frozen maple mousse is a favorite—are made daily.

The heart of this rustic lodge is the lobby, a dramatic two-story room with a huge granite fireplace. Comfortable chairs made from gnarled tree limbs, handforged iron hoop chandeliers, and an inner balcony around three sides add interest to this noble room.

The Hotel du Nord has its own private beach, sun deck, and pier overlooking Sister Bay, which is an ideal point from which to explore the delights of this beautiful peninsula.

HOTEL DU NORD, North Bay Shore Dr., Sister Bay, Wis. 54234; (414) 854-4221; Keyes and Ardis Fletcher, Innkeepers. A handsome hotel in the style of a rustic French-Canadian lodge overlooking Green Bay. Open from late May through Thanksgiving. Twenty-six rooms, cottages and villas, all with private baths. Room rate $26 to $38 single or double; cottages and villas $47 to $60 double occupancy, $70 for 4 in cottages. Complimentary continental breakfast. Dining room, open to public, serves dinner only Monday through Saturday. Huge Sunday brunch. Thanksgiving buffet dinner. Children welcome; no pets. No credit cards. Private beach, swimming, fishing, rowboats for guests, recreation room with indoor games. Sightseeing in surrounding area. Golf, tennis nearby.

DIRECTIONS: From Green Bay, Wis., take Rte. 57 north to Sister Bay. Hotel is 1 mile north of village.